THE DREAM OF REASON

JENNY GEORGE
THE DREAM OF REASON

COPPER CANYON PRESS

PORT TOWNSEND, WASHINGTON

Copper Canyon Press is in residence at Fort Worden State Park in Port Townsend, Washington, under the auspices of Centrum. Centrum is a gathering place for artists and creative thinkers from around the world, students of all ages and backgrounds, and audiences seeking extraordinary cultural enrichment.

LIBRARY OF CONGRESS CATALOGING-IN-PUBLICATION DATA

Names: George, Jenny, author.
Title: The dream of reason / Jenny George.
Description: Port Townsend, Washington : Copper Canyon Press, [2018] |
    Includes bibliographical references.
Identifiers: LCCN 2017045065 | ISBN 9781556595196 (softcover : acid-free paper)
Classification: LCC PS3607.E66295 A6 2018 | DDC 811/.6—dc23
LC record available at https://lccn.loc.gov/2017045065

98765432 FIRST PRINTING

COPPER CANYON PRESS

Post Office Box 271

Port Townsend, Washington 98368

www.coppercanyonpress.org

For Kate Carr

In 1799 the Spanish painter Francisco Goya created an etching called *El sueño de la razón produce monstruos.* The title has two English translations. The common one is *The sleep of reason produces monsters.* But it can also be translated *The dream of reason produces monsters.*

CONTENTS

THE DREAM OF REASON

Origins of Violence

There is a hole.
In the hole is everything
people will do
to each other.

The hole goes down and down.
It has many rooms
like graves and like graves
they are all connected.

Roots hang from the dirt
in craggy chandeliers.
It's not clear
where the hole stops

beginning and where
it starts to end.
It's warm and dark down there.
The passages multiply.

There are ballrooms.
There are dead ends.
The air smells of iron and
crushed flowers.

People will do anything.
They will cut the hands off children.
Children will do anything—

In the hole is everything.

I

Threshold Gods

I saw a bat in a dream and then later that week
I saw a real bat, crawling on its elbows
across the porch like a goblin.
It was early evening. I want to ask about death.

But first I want to ask about flying.

The swimmers talk quietly, standing waist-deep in the dark lake.
It's time to come in but they keep talking quietly.
Above them, early bats driving low over the water.
From here the voices are undifferentiated.
The dark is full of purring moths.

Think of it—to navigate by adjustment, by the beauty
of adjustment. All those shifts and echoes.
The bats veer and dive. Their eyes are tiny golden fruits.
They capture the moths in their teeth.

Summer is ending. The orchard is carved with the names of girls.
Wind fingers the leaves softly, like torn clothes.
Remember, desire was the first creature
that flew from the crevice
back when the earth and the sky were pinned together
like two rocks.

Now, I open the screen door and there it is—
a leather change purse
moving across the floorboards.

But in the dream you were large and you opened
the translucent hide of your body
and you folded me

in your long arms. And held me for a while.
As a bat might hold a small, dying bat. As the lake
holds the night upside down in its mouth.

Rehearsal

Another morning, raw sun on the snow—
the snow melted back in places, exposing the yellow grass.
I almost forget what shame is, the birds
coming down from the trees onto the wet, releasing earth.
They take quick, strategic bites of it—what only they can see:
seeds, tiny husks of insects frozen to transparency.
Then they fly off all at once, a mysterious agreement.
The great event—has it already occurred? Or is it waiting
in the future and we are standing fragile in front of it?
Or is it now, today—the snow crawling imperceptibly back
from the grass, the sun burning a white hole in the sky?

Everything Is Restored

He swallows the last spoonful
of prunes, their soft rapture
in his mouth. Then the jar
is washed under play of light,
then the boy's mouth
is wiped with a cloth.
He squalls for a moment, then
stops. Everything is restored.
Chime of spoon in the sink.
The boy is lifted out of his seat,
legs swimming in the slow
element. A small seal.
The kitchen ebbs and flows,
sleek afternoon sunshine.

Now the boy is placed
in his crib, now he is slipping
into the silvery minnows
of dreams, a disorder of shine,
particles of motion flickering
beneath the surface.
Harm will come. It's the kind of knowledge
that ruptures and won't
repair—an ocean that keeps
on breaking.

The day moves with the gradual logic
of drowning. Evening fills the house.
Oh, where are you? Where are you going?
The mother folds up the ocean
and shuts it in a cupboard.

Death of a Child

This is how a child dies:
His breath
curdles. His hands
soften, apricots
heavy on their branches.

I can't explain it.
I can't explain it.

On the walk back to the car
even the stones in the yards
are burning. Far overhead
in the dead orchard of space
a star explodes
and then collapses
into a black door.

This is the afterlife, but
I'm not dead. I'm just
here in this field.

2

It made a boy-shaped hole
and filled—

the way a crushed hand fills
suddenly up
with new pain,

or a well put down
taps the liquid silt.

The center pours
toward the surface.

Now the hand is given
to the earth.
The mouth draws up
clay
and drinks.

3

There's something uneasy in the field.
A wake. A ripple in the cloth.
We see the green corn moving
but not the thing that moves it.
The atoms of our bodies turn
bright gold and silky. Aimed
at death, we live. We keep on
doing this. Night unfolds helplessly
into day. Beyond the field are more
fields and through them, too—
this current. What is it? Where
is it going? Did you see it? Can you
catch it? Can you kill it? Can you hold
it still? Can you hold it still forever?

4

The conductor's baton hovers
for a moment in the alert
silence (a silence that leans forward
saying *Now...! Now...!*) and then it drops
into the chasm.

Sound enters the bodies
of all the people simultaneously,
calling them to feel together
an unconcealed fear, a cup over-
flowing, a sense of absolute love
vibrating in the dark passages—
the long-ago cry of pain
and the crack of light
coming in through the bars.

The Gesture of Turning a Mask Around

1

—so this god is only wood
and holes,
a blank,

like the moon's unlit side,
the side without grammar—

2

I stand alone under the stars,
audience to an immense quiet.

Or, not
quite alone. Something regards me
through an invisible opening.

3

If violence were obsolete—

If violence were obsolete (but it is not
obsolete)—

4

And the smell of the garden, wet-
blooded and heavy, like the sea
if the sea were earth.
A warm wind rises off the surface.

The hydrangea's blooms are big
as human heads among the leaves,
white and glowing faintly
from within their deep alcoves.

5

The opposite of language is not silence
but space.

It's dawn; the dark unjoins
and drifts off into light.
I enter the house and see
with astonishment the difference
between my rooms.

Troubles

The morning turns transparent, then
suddenly alive, the way a dream lifts
in stages from a body. Down in the orchard
mist glows like glass. These are my fields,
but still—I'm in the far country.
The trees are full of staring crows.
After we die, our lives take up no space at all.
The same is true of love. The black structures
of the cattle have been carried away in trucks.
What troubles the grass now is just wind.

Spring

Speckled egg, brown egg, or sky blue with black marks—

Having broken once, the world re-forms
in miniature.
Over and over, in the nest
between two limbs; in the hollow of grass
at a marsh edge.

It's relentless, the way it keeps trying
to return.
Joy
Joy
Joy

Encyclopedia of the Dead

A body was removed from the house.
Only in the northern regions were bodies
twined together to make rains of autumn.
As far south as the coast the dead were able
to live on sandy beaches in summer.
The force of the sea was highly desirable.
In winter months when storm winds blew
makeshift shelters were erected, rounded hulls
sometimes plain, sometimes in the forms
of animals and monsters. The flesh of the dead
was secluded, long and ribbonlike.
They were both in danger and dangerous.
Dishes were often hollowed out of pieces
of old dried fish. Spoons and ladles
were placed on the beach (emphasis
on symmetry, neatness). Over most of the coast
there was a very great fear of the dead.
Elsewhere, trinket boxes served as coffins.

II

The Sleeping Pig

It is easy to love a pig in a nightgown.
See how he sleeps, white flannel
straining his neck at the neckhole.
His body swells and then deflates.
The gown is nothing to be ashamed of, only
the white clay of moonlight smeared
over his hulk, original clothing, the milk
of his loneliness. The flickering candle
of a dream moves his warty eyelids.
All sleeping things are children.

The Traveling Line

The sun on their backs is a stroke of burning gold.
They smell the bright dust of the yard.
The pigs are loaded onto trucks.
The pigs are prodded through a passage.
They roll their many eyes.
They see the hind legs of the one ahead.
They call to one another like birds.
The pigs become a traveling line.
Moving up the ramp the fever rises.
There is the clank of metal.
They hold still inside confusion.
A current passes through their bodies.
Blood comes from their mouths in strings.
By the ankles they are swiftly inverted.
Blood comes from their mouths in strings.
A current passes through their bodies.
They hold still inside confusion.
There is the clank of metal.
Moving up the ramp the fever rises.
The pigs become a traveling line.
They call to one another like birds.
They see the hind legs of the one ahead.
They roll their many eyes.
The pigs are prodded through a passage.
The pigs are loaded onto trucks.
They smell the bright dust of the yard.
The sun on their backs is a stroke of burning gold.

The Belt

After she heaved all day against the boards
of her enclosure, after she panted so long
that foam bloomed on her lips, after the sun
sharpened like fumes over the field and shadows
began to climb out of the earth,
he unbuckled his belt and fed the leather
between her teeth, the big tongue soft
as a sea creature, saying Here
        Bite down, girl—

I come to give you something, and the gift
is your own strength, returned to you
as surrender

—and she mouthed hard
and the calf came out like jelly, inert
and cooling on the trampled straw.
It was dusk. High above us
swallows found their holes in the tower of hay.
A few minutes later, she stood.
Drank a little water from the trough.
His belt where she'd chewed it
was like chewed bread. And how
did you imagine mercy would look?

Notes on Pigs

A pig has eyelashes.
The pig's eyelashes function like our own eyelashes,
          but have a different meaning.
A pig who cares about her looks is absurd.
A pig does not take a long evening bath, with a glass
          of sparkling grapefruit juice set on the porcelain ledge.
Many people live near animals.
A person who cares about a pig is a rare thing.
Neither a pig nor a person is invincible.
A pig is a tasty thing, when killed and cooked.
A person dressed in a pig costume is trying to be funny.
Pigs have superior eyesight.
A pig can see the silver belly of a plane moving across the sky.
Or a beetle crawling up a fence post.
Certain pink tulips, when the sun hits them, have the color
          of a clean pig.
A pig can only give birth to a person in a dream.
When a pig dies, it is either mourned by other pigs or not.

Obstacles to Handling

> Many common elements of the processing system
> present obstacles for the livestock.

Rustling cloth.
Sun glinting off a metal bar.
A hallway that turns at a right angle.
A man in an orange hat standing in a new place.
The clanking of chains.
Shadow of chains hanging.
A rod coming toward the front of the neck.

> The fears become large; they rise
> from their objects and enter space
> like a kind of halo.
> And at the center, a monument
> of pure stillness, an uncrossable field…

A hose hissing.
A gap of more than four inches.
Darkness coming out of a hole in the floor.

Ears

The pig is already dead.
It hangs from the ankle,
slumped as light
through a heavy curtain.
Draped onto the slab.
One ear folded like a lily
under the ample head,
pressed nearly in half,
silent origami.
The other ear,
large as a trumpet flower,
turned open as if to receive
the sound of a distant thing
approaching—
a train through fall fields,
an insect in forgotten rafters
droning its thin scarves of sound.
The one ear
bent shut, weighted
under the pig's last greatness.
The other, supple horn,
listens outward, catches
the squeal of the gate hinge.

The Farrowing Crate

> A cage-like gestation unit large enough to hold a sow
> but too narrow to permit it to turn around.

For months she points in one direction,
a zeppelin bumbling toward the rising sun.
She drinks from her spigot.
She is big as a doorstep.
They say she doesn't know she cannot turn around.

When I turned nine my mother hung
a piñata from a tree, and spun me—
blinded, dizzy with anticipation—
until my heart was a blur, then let me loose
to strike at the thing.
It took ten minutes of hard beating
to split it, and then turned out
to be filled not with candy
but cheap Mexican toys.

They say her brain does not conceive
of turning. But after farrowing,
back in the pen with the others,
she'll circle herself for days
trying to bite her own tail.

Portrait of a Pig as a Bird

Small, bitten wings ornament the head.

Song whistles from the nostrils:
breathing in is thrushes, breathing out is cranes.
The eyes are black seeds.
There is a crooked delicacy in the legs.

The pig is a bird of mud.
It nests in wallows and beds of muck,
brooding for open sky.

Flocks of wild pigs migrating
across fields of goldenrod
used to bruise the land each September.
Early explorers wrote in their diaries
of a flush of pigs darkening the hills, pigs
as far as the eye could see.
You can jab your prod in any direction
and get one.

An enclosed pig gives us cagey looks.
Something flightless is cramped in its heart.

One-Way Gate

I was moving the herd from the lower pasture
to the loading pen up by the road.
It was cold and their mouths steamed like torn bread.
The gate swung on its wheel, knocking at the herd
as they pushed through. They stomped
and pocked the freezing mud with their hooves.
This was January. I faced backward into the hard year.
The herd faced forward as the herd always does,
muscling through the lit pane of winter air.

It could have been any gate, any moment when things go
one way and not the other—an act of tenderness
or a small, cruel thing done with a pocketknife.
A child being born. Or the way we move
from sleeping to dreams, as a river flows uneasy under ice.

Of course, nothing can ever be returned to exactly.
In the pen the herd nosed the fence and I forked them hay.
A few dry snowflakes swirled the air. The truck would be there
in an hour. Hey, good girl. Go on. Get on, girl.

The Veld

Lions were near the cattle.
Big, dusty creatures, flies orbiting their heads.
The herd was tense—a current passing
from body to body through the stamped grass.
The lions watched from the heat,
flicking their tails.

But this morning the cows
are undisturbed, mild in their cool stalls.
A calf, still with her mother, licks my arm
when I lean in to stroke her, the tongue
already rough and strong.

I slide back the barn door. The day advances—
the earth's low vapors burning into light,
the herd moving out over the open land,
hawks circling, air shimmering with insects
hatched up from wet grass, the stink
of manure and gasoline—all life mixing
in threat and hunger
under the spring sun.

Influence

The quiet handling of pigs produces quieter pigs.

True, we mold the world.
Something passes through our hands—
a pig, a person, clay or alloy,
some living material—and the handling
shapes the thing.
I plump the down pillows into blimps.
I split a melon and two neat halves fall away.
Things proceed from us.
This illusion is smooth and enduring.

But in certain rare moments, the gears kink,
sputter, and reverse. Then objects
flash us with their genius.
Fingers twined in yarn become yarn.
A knife's intention travels up the arm.
And the pigs—hushed, breathing
calmly in their pens—quiet us into handlers.

Vision

Last night, in the deeper hours, I found myself
watched over by the large, single eye of a cow,
which hung above my bed, its veins
rich and elaborate as a chandelier.
I felt visited. I felt seen into the very stations
of my bones—the kind of seeing that has
no purpose beyond its own canny radiance.
The eye was not altogether unwelcome.
It tinged my sleep with a quality of vividness,
like dreaming under a wakeful star, or a jellyfish
streaming through night's suspension.
Between breaths, the bed's feathers rustled.
Outside, other windows in other houses
glowed with their own electric dreams.

First Day of Lent

You make room for the silence
and so it fills you, comes in like the sea
through a great door.
What you give away returns.
The two halves of the world.

I fill the grain bucket with grain.
The water bucket with water.

I find a calf dead in the barn
—heavy as a sleeping boy—
and I bury him under the field,
down where the rain is kept.

The River

The lambs I curled like twins
and laid into their boats. I stuffed their ears
with the woolly sound of sleep.
The pigs I showered with white carnations.
The cows I placed cut branches over, green parasols
fluttering on the stems. All the dead
becalmed in their vessels, sent onto the river.
The river was a murmur of many boats drifting.
Petals in the eddies, creak of prow against stern…
The parade grew large between the banks.
Then there were only boats, boats
and the sound of water beneath them.

Vaudeville

The pigs hang in rows like pink overcoats.
Their slaughter is fresh, a rosy blush—
as if chorus girls have only just
stepped out of them,
leaving the empty garments
swaying on their hooks.

Westward Expansion

Take the prairie, emptied
Of cattle, those great bellows of dust;

Take the tainted creeks and empty their pinks
And coppers into the river.

The throats of cows, empty them—
Low sounds rising in blood, forming

One common chord that hangs in the sky
With the charge of a summer storm.

Take Oxford, Iowa—the already-empty buildings,
Storefronts stacked with school chairs;

Take the brain, the eyes, spinal cord, and nerves.
A pair of lungs opening into air and then

Collapsing, returning to us through history.
Take a newborn calf and wind it

In a piece of cloth, it is no different
From any organ lifted out of a body—

III

New World

There are no slaughterhouses.
The glittering river has seeped
back into the healed earth.
The fields are wrung dry
and laid out like a flag.

There are no feedlots for fattening.
Steel chutes stand blank
and open, rendering only a grain
of sunlight, an empty wind.

In this great stillness,
which is neither happy
nor unhappy, a fly
does his tedious business.
The flank of an eating animal shudders.

At night, the stars fall from their Bethlehems
and land, sputtering in the fields
like bottle rockets.
To the animals standing half-asleep
these are only angels
to be taken lightly.
Their hides grow long and prehistoric,
fed on the rich darkness.
They've become their own slumbering houses,
ovens banked and keeping.

In the morning, the sun may rise.
Who knows.
There is nothing to be longed for.

The Cave

Someone strikes a match. Briefly
the earth is illuminated.
Then it goes out, just the drifting flare of memory.
But our eyes hold it—for a while
it will be all we can see,
the dark will stream with it, the nerves
will salvage back the light until they can't
and we are bodies again.

Sword-Swallower

I

The soul enters the body
through the mouth.

So the legends say.

I say: the soul enters
through childhood.

2

A barn with its doors left open
fills with night swallows—
In the hayloft
certain dark sections
flicker with movement,
the dimension of depth.

Finally, stillness. The moon—
a threshing tool
revealed in the diminished light.
The glint of its blade.

And the earth under a black quilt.

3

Sleep: that ancient union
of death with its body.

The child sleeps.
As in—the child returns
to the time before her body.

But the earth always adjusts.
A blueness pools in the shadows.
Dawn pierces her
with its strange dream—
The birds open their throats, cry out—

4

Before language, there was just
the peculiar house of nerves.
Now the world is buried in me, to the hilt.
I know exactly
what I want.

The sun burns off the mist.
I take my violence out over the field.

The Drowning

She sank and died—the girl
from out of town that summer.
They pulled her body
like waterweed, then winter came,
enclosed the lake in glass, and sealed
the dark cavern of our questions.

We skated on the frozen shell.
All around, the mountains glittered,
chained in ice. The lake was pale blue
and cracked with stars—
We lay on our backs
acquiring a sense of the ordinary.
With the cold driving into our skulls
we watched our breaths rise
and vanish upward into the depths.

Winter Variations

Four p.m., a snowy forest; stillness.
Our skis hiss on the ice grains.

A vole darts over the surface, black and elegant.
In a vast theater: one note played on a piano.
It vanishes under a drift.

Briefly the trees hold the light in their arms.

Reprieve

Before the insects start to grind their million bodies,
before impulse scatters the deer into the trees,
before desire:
>   there's a rest.
The dawn and the day observe each other.

The herd begins to move over the field, one shared dream
of grass and wind.
The small stones of their hooves in the stony field.

I've exhausted my cruelty.
I've arrived at myself again.
The sun builds a slow house inside my house,
touching the stilled curtains, the bottoms of cups
left out on the table.

The Dream of Reason

1 Self-Portrait

A house
with three stories.
In the basement, monsters.
The upper floors were empty.
No furniture, nothing.
I had a magic pebble
that I needed to hide.
But where?
Woke in a room
with the bed breathing.
Each day the same
scandal—this body.
These teeth and hands.

2 The Miniature Bed

A miniature bed, and in it two tiny people
not sleeping, not able to sleep because
a small lie has flowered between them,
fragile as a new, white crocus.
The miniature bed holds them like a miniature boat
making its slow, true course to morning.
These tiny people, thoughts thrumming like mice,
are quiet as the lie blooms over them
in the night, fanning its moth petals,
becoming to them like a moon hovering
over their bed, a moon they might almost touch
with their miniature hands, if they weren't certain
that one wrong gesture might break
the spindles of their small world, if their hearts
were not drops of trembling quicksilver,
if they were brave, if they could see
that small is no smaller than big, that thimbles
are deep as oceans for any god, they might even
touch each other then, opening the dark,
like a match, the sun's flaring.

3 Harvest

The fields are a book of uses.
Near the house
a combine takes the corn down
in long rows.
Dust rises up and replaces itself.
A quick net of starlings
drops to the furrows
and sunshine pours like polished grain
onto the feeding earth,
this country.

In the kitchen, milk streams
from the gallon
thin and fresh as luck.
We flourish.
All around us, things flourish.
Cows strain the fence with their abundance.
The herd makes a sound like swelling.

Out in the cut field
birds clean the fallen cobs
into sets of teeth.

4 Sonnet for Lost Teeth

The combines were tearing off the field's clothes.
It was August, haying season. My tooth
was loose, a snag in the clam of my mouth.
I worked it like a pearl. I'd been out of school
for sixty days. In the sweat of the barn
I watched him shoot the calf in the head.
He wiped the hide gently, like cleaning his glasses.
Overnight, I grew a beard so I wouldn't
have to get married. I let my feet go black
from burned grasses. *It never gets easier*
he said, kicking straw over the blood patch.
She went down so quiet it was almost
sad. Later, when my tooth fell out, I buried it
under my pillow and it grew into money.

5 Talisman

Waiting for the school bus you find
the femur of a baby animal
on the ground. You carry
that femur in your pocket
the entire morning and touch it
secretly through the cloth.
When the teacher asks
a question you don't raise
your hand but quietly
wrap your fingers around
the thin shape, that bone
without a mother.

6 On Waking

Half of everything is invisible.
A river drifts below the river.
A gesture lost in the body.
Wind moves through the open
windows of the trees.

Beyond the day, another day.

Dreamed I was drowning
my mother's silk laundry
in the river,
kneeling on the wet rocks.
Back and forth I drowned it
in the gray clouds...

7 Eros

Each year fish run the green vein of the river.
The bones of skunks lie buried in the riverbank
upside down, waiting for rain.

From a fragment of a Greek statue
you can tell the posture of the whole god.
A skeleton has the same intelligence.

So that when a girl discovers it,
loosened by summer rain, surfaced
like a white instrument in the grass,
she suddenly knows how to take it up
and shake the strange rhythms from it like castanets.

8 A Childhood

The horse had been beaten and flies
crawled excited on the beat marks.
He held still in the sunblazed pasture.
For a few minutes I stood at the wire fence.
He was aware of me, but he did not turn—
except his eye, slightly. He listened
through the many ears of the grasses.
A jay made a hole in the air with its cry.
Everywhere, invisible as heat, the gods
married each other and went to war.
The excitement of it vibrated in the flies.
As if we both were standing still
inside some greater, more violent motion.

Revelation

When the brain stem of a frog
is expertly snipped, the body sac slit,
skin pinned back in flaps and then
the jellies of the chest arranged
to reveal the heart, the heart itself
can be unfastened, clipped, lifted
like a gray pearl on the tip of a knife,
still trembling, and dropped in a beaker of water
where it beats alone
for the lifetime of a minute, sends plumes
of blood into suspension, then beats itself clean,
keeps on beating without brain
or aim, a small fist tightening,
forgetting, and tightening again.
The opened frog rests coolly on a wax tablet.
Gradually the heart in its jar drifts toward stillness.

My father showed me this one day
at his laboratory, afterward wiping
his scalpel dry with alcohol. I'm not sorry
for the frog. I'm not sorry to know this.

Spring

A devastation has occurred. Does it matter
what it was? Who commanded it?

Or, if it split the ground
with its own energies?

The bare moon rises over the orchard.
Inside the house, the curtains move a little.

A lone bullfrog bellows from the woods—a single, wet note.
Almost a bark, but deeper.
Sexual. Discordant.
Night after night, this astonishing sound.

Mnemonic

I forgot the prairie because it stood
so still. I forgot the clouds because
they were always moving. I forgot
the taste of water because it lay quietly
inside the taste of everything.

I forgot a childhood when it disappeared
through a hole in itself. Later, mushrooms
emerged from the damp soil.

The way to keep something is to forget it.
Then it goes to an enormous place.

Grass grows to the horizon like hair.
In the sky a cloud goes on naming
and unnaming itself.

Intelligence

How easily the deer move between
the field and the woods.
Only we know a thing by its periphery:
the meadow edged with trees.
Or happiness with its horizon of pain.
From inside the house I watch them grazing,
their pooled memory guiding them
into the shade, then into the grass again.

Easter

They say it is the soul that rises, not the body.
But the body does rise—

Overhead, in the spring wind
trees are touching each other
with quiet gestures.

Winter: the buried forms.

Then the snow drawn under the trees, then the rings
of snow gone entirely, spring rains—
and the trees green and bending.
They have taken up
the rain and used it.
The air is fresh, smelling of wood.

What will be first to emerge?
The brain, pushing its murderous bulb
through the mud? The heart? No—
the heart is last to rise.
The first to emerge is the image.

NOTES

"The Gesture of Turning a Mask Around" is the title of an essay by Vilém Flusser. The poem also references *Twenty-One Love Poems* by Adrienne Rich:

> such hands might carry out an unavoidable violence
> with such restraint, with such a grasp
> of the range and limits of violence
> that violence ever after would be obsolete.

The language of "Encyclopedia of the Dead" is taken from a single page of *Encyclopaedia Britannica,* 1978. The order of words and phrases has been changed. No words were added.

"The Belt" contains a line fragment from *Oedipus at Colonus* by Sophocles.

Epigraphs to "Obstacles to Handling," "The Farrowing Crate," and "Influence" are from manuals on industrial livestock management.

ACKNOWLEDGMENTS

Grateful acknowledgment is given to the following journals in which these poems, sometimes in earlier versions, first appeared:

Beloit Poetry Journal: "Sword-Swallower"

BLOOM: "The Sleeping Pig"

Boston Review: "Obstacles to Handling"

Chaparral: "Ears"

Cimarron Review: "Influence" and "The Miniature Bed"

The Collagist: "Portrait of a Pig as a Bird" and "The Traveling Line"

Copper Nickel: "Everything Is Restored"

Crab Orchard Review: "Sonnet for Lost Teeth" and "Vaudeville"

failbetter: "Death of a Child (3)" and "Westward Expansion"

FIELD: "The Farrowing Crate" and "Threshold Gods"

Four Way Review: "Death of a Child (1)," "Reprieve," and "The River"

Gulf Coast: "Mnemonic"

Indiana Review: "Encyclopedia of the Dead"

Narrative: "A Childhood," "Easter," and "The Gesture of Turning a Mask Around"

North American Review: "Origins of Violence"

Painted Bride Quarterly: "Notes on Pigs"

Ploughshares: "The Drowning"

Poetry Quarterly: "First Day of Lent"

Prodigal: "Intelligence"

RHINO: "One-Way Gate"

Shenandoah: "The Belt" and "Revelation"

For the gifts of time and financial resources, I thank the Bread Loaf Writers' Conference, the Dorothy Sargent Rosenberg Memorial Fund, Hedgebrook Writers' Residency, the MacDowell Colony, the Ragdale Foundation, the Vermont Studio Center, and Yaddo.

For their support, I thank my parents, Katie and Stephen George.

For their wisdom and encouragement, I thank: Tara Brown, Matt Donovan, Erik Ehn, Maude Foster, Kay Hagan, Dana Levin, Terri Rolland, Candice Stover, Arthur Sze, and Michael Wiegers. For her vision and generosity: Louise Glück.

I am deeply grateful to Jan Arsenault.

And for her brilliance and love, I thank my sister, Madeleine George. This book would not exist without her.

ABOUT THE AUTHOR

Jenny George lives in Santa Fe, New Mexico. She is a winner of the Discovery/Boston Review Poetry Prize, and her poems have appeared in *FIELD*, *Gulf Coast*, *Narrative*, and *Ploughshares*, among other publications. She received her MFA from the University of Iowa Writers' Workshop.

Poetry is vital to language and living. Since 1972, Copper Canyon Press has published extraordinary poetry from around the world to engage the imaginations and intellects of readers, writers, booksellers, librarians, teachers, students, and donors.

WE ARE GRATEFUL FOR THE MAJOR SUPPORT PROVIDED BY:

Anonymous

Jill Baker and Jeffrey Bishop

Donna and Matt Bellew

John Branch

Diana Broze

Sarah and Tim Cavanaugh

Janet and Les Cox

Mimi Gardner Gates

Linda Gerrard and Walter Parsons

Gull Industries, Inc.
on behalf of Ruth and William True

The Trust of Warren A. Gummow

Steven Myron Holl

Phil Kovacevich and Eric Wechsler

Lakeside Industries, Inc.
on behalf of Jeanne Marie Lee

Maureen Lee and Mark Busto

Rhoady Lee and Alan Gartenhaus

Ellie Mathews and Carl Youngmann as
The North Press

Anne O'Donnell and John Phillips

Petunia Charitable Fund and advisor
Elizabeth Hebert

Suzie Rapp and Mark Hamilton

Jill and Bill Ruckelshaus

Cynthia Lovelace Sears and
Frank Buxton

Kim and Jeff Seely

Catherine Eaton Skinner and
David Skinner

Dan Waggoner

Austin Walters

Barbara and Charles Wright

The dedicated interns and faithful
volunteers of Copper Canyon Press

TO LEARN MORE ABOUT UNDERWRITING COPPER CANYON PRESS TITLES,
PLEASE CALL 360-385-4925 EXT. 103

Lannan Literary Selections

For two decades Lannan Foundation has supported the publication and distribution of exceptional literary works. Copper Canyon Press gratefully acknowledges their support.

LANNAN LITERARY SELECTIONS 2018

Sherwin Bitsui, *Dissolve*

Jenny George, *The Dream of Reason*

Ha Jin, *A Distant Center*

Aimee Nezhukumatathil, *Oceanic*

C.D. Wright, *Casting Deep Shade*

RECENT LANNAN LITERARY SELECTIONS FROM COPPER CANYON PRESS

Josh Bell, *Alamo Theory*

Marianne Boruch, *Cadaver, Speak*

Olena Kalytiak Davis, *The Poem She Didn't Write and Other Poems*

Michael Dickman, *Green Migraine*

John Freeman, *Maps*

Deborah Landau, *The Uses of the Body*

Maurice Manning, *One Man's Dark*

Rachel McKibbens, *blud*

W.S. Merwin, *The Lice*

Camille Rankine, *Incorrect Merciful Impulses*

Roger Reeves, *King Me*

Paisley Rekdal, *Imaginary Vessels*

Brenda Shaughnessy, *So Much Synth*

Richard Siken, *War of the Foxes*

Frank Stanford, *What About This: Collected Poems of Frank Stanford*

Ocean Vuong, *Night Sky with Exit Wounds*

Javier Zamora, *Unaccompanied*

Ghassan Zaqtan (translated by Fady Joudah), *The Silence That Remains*

The Chinese character for poetry is made up of two
parts: "word" and "temple." It also serves as pressmark for
Copper Canyon Press.

The poems are set in Adobe Caslon Pro. Headings are set in Quarto.
Printed on archival-quality paper using soy-based inks.
Book design and composition by Phil Kovacevich.